Contents

Introduction

Anyone who walks into my class or opens this book is already an artist. My job is not to make you paint like me, but to help you develop the skills to express your unique viewpoint.

I began oil painting at the age of ten and have loved it ever since. I have no doubt that you will too. It's no fluke that oil paint, which came into regular use in the 15th century, is still the most popular painting medium. Artists love the rich, gloopy nature of the paint, combined with the fact that it can be used in an infinite number of ways.

Famous for its slow drying time, oil paint is ideal for soft blending. Diluted as thin as watercolour, it makes rich, transparent glazes. Using a palette knife or hog-hair brush, we can create mountainous textures of paint up to an inch thick.

Unique to oil paint is the amazing ability to retain the three-dimensional shape of the artist's mark. Each brushstroke is like a little time capsule, showing us the exact touch and speed of the painter's hand.

Those who see oil painting as a difficult option, suitable only for the serious professional, have usually been put off by the mystery surrounding drying times, or confusing rules such as 'fat over lean'. In fact, the rules of oil painting are very simple. Once you know them, you are free to do almost anything while producing works that will last for generations.

For me, the best thing of all about oil paint is its forgiving nature. I'm one of those people who never get it right first time. With oil paint, you can scrape it off and repaint as many times as you like.

Starting out as a painter, you will learn more from doing ten small paintings than labouring away on one huge canvas. In the step-by-step demonstrations, I give as clear instructions as I can, but remember that most artists are a touch rebellious. If you feel like tinkering with the techniques or substituting subjects, I won't tell.

The aim here is not to produce ten gallery paintings in a uniform style. We will be tackling lots of different subjects and using a whole range of techniques. Give them all a try and discard the ones that don't feel natural. By the end of the book, you won't be afraid of any subject and you'll have some really exciting approaches up your sleeve.

The approach to painting presented in this book is just one of many. It is my approach, developed through emulating great art of the past and based on my love of light, colour and paint texture. Take all you can from these pages, but borrow from other sources too. Don't be afraid of losing your artistic identity in learning from others. Your own personality will always shine through.

There are a couple of unexpected benefits to becoming an oil painter. One is the close and supportive community of artists you will discover in your local area and online. The other is the opening of your eyes to the beauty of the world around you. It comes with a warning. You might find yourself, driving around town, distracted by glorious reflected light from a brick wall.

Regardless of the stage in life you are taking up painting, there will be challenges and triumphs aplenty. It is not unusual for the absolute beginner to produce a scintillating, lively piece of art, while the veteran is still capable of something perfectly correct, but quite dull. I encourage you to embrace the unpredictable nature of art, have fun and take some risks. Your growth as an artist is guaranteed when you are willing to squeeze out some paint, put in some 'brush miles' and reach beyond your current skills.

Norman

Materials and Equipment

When you start oil painting, there are a number of essentials you need. The amount of choice in an art shop can be quite overwhelming, so this section lists the absolute basics required, from paints to palettes and other items. Oil paints are expensive, but fretting over the cost of oil paint and squeezing out meagre amounts will lead to stingy-looking paintings.

Oil paints

When buying oil paint, you will notice two grades – 'student' and 'artist's' – with a jump in cost between the two. To start with, I recommend buying student grade such as Winton by Winsor & Newton.

Some colours have the word 'hue' after their name. 'Cadmium red hue' looks like cadmium red but is actually made from cheaper, weaker pigments. For this reason, an affluent artist will prefer artist's quality paint for the cadmium colours, but the main thing is that you squeeze out plenty of paint and use it up without a second thought.

This is my recommended palette, with alternatives listed alongside:

- Titanium white – large tube (7fl oz/200ml)
- Cadmium yellow pale (light)
- Cadmium red (or cadmium scarlet/ cadmium red light)
- Permanent alizarin crimson (or permanent rose)
- Phthalo blue (or ultramarine, sometimes called French ultramarine)
- Viridian hue (or Winsor green/ phthalo green, but not artist's quality viridian)
- Yellow ochre
- Burnt sienna
- Ivory black (or lamp black).

Supports and grounds

The 'support' is the material we paint on. The 'ground' is a layer of primer we apply to the support to stop the paint from sinking in. Wood or stretched canvas are traditional supports for oil painting. Though we will often refer to the painting surface as the 'canvas', we will actually be using hardboard (Masonite). This is available from your local wood merchant and is easily cut to size with a craft knife. Common sizes used in this book are 10 x 12in (25 x 30cm), and 10 x 10in (25 x 25cm).

Acrylic gesso is by far the handiest ground to apply to hardboard. Use a household paintbrush and give it two or three coats, brushing in random directions. If your hardboard has a rough side and a smooth side, try to avoid the rough side as it tends to overwhelm your brushmarks. These days, remarkably cheap canvases and canvas boards are widely available. As they are, many of them are too absorbent, but give them another coat of acrylic gesso and they will be fine.

The tools used by an oil painter.

If you find yourself with lots of leftover oil paint, you can create an interesting surface by applying it to an already primed board. Use brushes and a palette knife to create the textures you like.

Working over old oil or acrylic paintings is an excellent idea and can create really interesting and unexpected effects. It is not advisable to use acrylic gesso over old oil paintings, as this layer will crack over time.

If the finished painting is likely to be stored somewhere damp, it's best to prime the back too, to prevent warping. You can bypass this step by buying 'white-faced hardboard'. The white side is ideal for the back of the painting, meaning you just need to prime the brown side and you're ready to roll.

Once dried, paintings on hardboard can be stacked together. Tape bubble wrap to the back of each painting to prevent them sticking together or damaging the impasto (thick paint).

Priming hardboard with acrylic gesso.

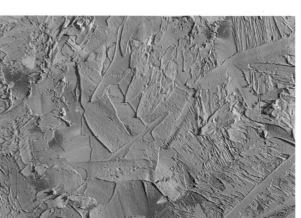

Primed hardboard covered in a textured surface of oil paint.

Bubble wrap on the back of paintings prevents damage to the surfaces of other paintings.

Brushes

There are three main shapes of brushes – rounds, flats and filberts. You will need at least 12 brushes of various sizes, preferably with long handles to keep you a comfortable distance from the canvas.

Hog hair is the traditional bristle for oil brushes. It gives distinctive brush-marks, ideal for big, bold strokes. I use hog-hair filberts for my larger brushes. Sizes 8, 6 and 4 were used for these paintings. When it comes to smaller details, a softer synthetic brush (such as the Ivory range from Rosemary & Co.) lays the paint on beautifully. No. 2 long flats and pointed rounds are a treat. The use of a No. 1 pointed round is permissible, but only in the last half hour of a painting!

Palette knife

A metal palette knife with a cranked handle is a great tool for mixing paint and cleaning off the palette. It is also used for various painting techniques. The most versatile are teardrop shaped knives such as the Winsor & Newton No. 21 (or Liquitex small No. 15).

Palettes

Any surface that is large enough (at least 16 x 12in/40 x 30cm), flat and non-absorbent will serve as a palette. The traditional wooden hand-held palette is kidney-shaped with a thumb-hole, allowing the artist to stand back and mix colours as they contemplate the canvas from a distance. To keep wooden palettes in beautiful condition, rub a spot of linseed oil into the surface after cleaning. If you have a table it can rest on, a piece of safety glass (thick, with safe edges) makes the perfect studio palette. It is a dream to clean. The underside can be painted grey (or put a piece of coloured paper underneath) so that you can see both light and dark colours clearly. Disposable palettes are convenient, but tend to be on the small side.

Other essentials

Other items you will need are a small dipper for holding solvent or painting medium. Suitable solvents include white spirit, turpentine, Zest-it (Europe), mineral spirits or Gamsol (USA). Solvent can be mixed with refined linseed oil to make your own medium.

Laying brushes down on the palette is messy; they can easily roll off and they take up mixing space – so you'll need a wide-mouthed jar for holding wet brushes. You can use a washed-out tin can for cleaning brushes, but beware of sharp edges!

Keep a stock of cotton rags or good-quality kitchen paper, which does not crumble when wet, close to hand. An old telephone directory can be useful for wiping your palette knife or oily brushes on when you have finished painting.

Filbert, long flat and pointed round brushes.

Easels

An easel is necessary to hold the painting vertically next to the subject so that you can make easy comparisons between the two. It also allows you to stand back to view the painting from a distance.

The metal sketching (or Field) easel is designed for outdoors but can also be used inside and takes up very little space. Avoid wooden sketching easels (or the very cheap aluminium ones), as they are too flimsy. The French easel, suitable for indoors and out, allows you to carry a wet palette in a useful drawer. A studio easel such as the radial easel is a sturdy investment. It can handle even large canvases with ease. Specialist pochade boxes are handy when doing small outdoor paintings.

Cleaning

At the end of a painting session, use your palette knife to scrape the piles of paint off your palette and wipe the surface with a rag. The paint can be discarded or scraped into piles, stored in a biscuit tin and kept for up to a few weeks in the freezer. I call this my 'palette mud', and it can be used for the next painting.

The better you clean your brushes, the longer they will last. If you are painting the next day, you can store them temporarily in a plastic bag in the fridge. For a proper clean, wipe them first on a telephone directory, then swirl them in solvent and wipe with a rag. A final step of cleaning on your palm with hand soap will remove the last residue of colour.

Dirty solvent should not be put down the drain but can be recycled for use in cleaning brushes. Pour it into a jar and wait for the sediment to settle to the bottom.

From left to right: radial, sketching and French easels. Front: pochade box.

Piles of paint stored in a tin for reuse.

Drawing

My approach to oil painting is very direct – get the big things down first and add details later. A careful pencil drawing at the outset can take too long and, having invested time in a careful drawing, an artist may not wish to spend the time making necessary changes. It is better to use a brush and diluted paint to draw the big shapes.

Drawing with paint

To start drawing with paint, hold the brush at the far end and stand well back from the canvas so that you can see the proportions at a glance. For large strokes, hold the brush underhand (thumb on top) and use the movement of your arm. For finer drawing, hold the brush like a pencil and use your fingers.

The big trick in drawing is seeing everything as flat shapes, rather like jigsaw pieces. Start with the big shapes and keep moving around the whole drawing. The first aim is not a lovely drawing but to get things in the right place within the canvas. Resist the urge to finish any part of the drawing, but erase and redraw until you are happy with the size and positioning of the objects on the canvas.

The next step is to use the following techniques to check what you have – and continue to check and adjust your shapes until the last minute of the painting.

Measurements and alignment

If you can find two distances in the subject that are the same, you know that they will also match on your painting. Done properly, this simple matching measurement is extremely reliable.

1. Working from an actual subject, hold a paintbrush in your outstretched hand with your elbow locked and one eye closed. Try not to tilt the brush forward to match the angle of the subject but do keep it parallel to the lenses of your glasses (whether you wear them or not). You can only rotate the brush like the hands of a clock.

2. Look for two large measurements in the subject, one vertical and one horizontal, which are the same. Closing one eye, align the brush tip with the top of the mug and slide your thumb down until it meets the bottom of the plate.

3. Still holding your thumb in position, rotate the brush horizontally and look for a matching measurement.

4. Don't take the measurement from the subject and transfer it directly onto the painting. Instead, remove your thumb and repeat the process on the painting. Placing the tip of the brush on the painting, use your thumb to measure the height.

5. Now compare this measurement to the width. If the vertical and horizontal measurements match, proceed with confidence. If not, adjust one or the other (or both) until they do.

6. You need things at the top of the drawing to line up with those at the bottom and things at the left to line up with those on the right. Use your paintbrush vertically or horizontally (or even at an angle) to find two things in the subject that line up. Then check that they also align in your painting.

Negative shapes

Any shape caught between or around objects is known as a negative shape. While drawing things can be hard, copying shapes is easy. Pay close attention to the kind of shapes outlined in orange (see bottom right) and you will find that the objects magically draw themselves.

Using a mirror

A mirror is the most useful tool of all for checking shapes and angles. Face away from your subject and hold a mirror roughly where your head was while you were painting, so that you can see the subject and the painting next to each other. Jump your eyes back and forth between the two, looking for the big differences in shapes or angles. Once you notice something, put the mirror down and correct your painting.

Light, Shade and Tone

Lines are magic. Since childhood, we have been able to create symbols using lines, which everyone recognizes. Yet those lines do not actually exist in nature. A line is the division between a light shape and a dark shape. To progress beyond drawing into painting, we need to move beyond lines into light and shade.

1A

1B

Whiter than white

As painters, we hope to create the illusion of light, yet if the brightest thing we have is white paint, how can we make the highlight on a teapot glow? (**1A**). While colour can certainly enhance the illusion, the real secret lies in the tonal values.

The only way to make one thing look light is by making everything else a little bit darker. The highlight on the teapot looks shiny because it is the only area of white paint in the whole painting. Compare the swatches at the bottom of **1B** and you will see that the highlight is the only patch of white paint in the whole painting. Even the white plate is darker.

Light and shade

Light is logical. It can't bend around corners; it can only go in straight lines. This means that every object lit by a single light source will have a light side and a dark side. Draw as badly as you like; if you can keep the light side light and the shadow side dark, you will have a three-dimensional object.

Let's have a look and see what light does when it meets an egg. Place an egg on a flat surface with the light coming from one side. Where it first strikes the egg is the lightest part – the highlight. As the surface curves away from the light, it turns into a halftone. The shadow side is the darkest and the surface on which the egg sits will have a cast shadow (**2A**).

Now take a piece of brightly coloured paper and hold it next to the shadow side of the egg. The wonderful colour you see

in the egg is reflected light. Squint your eyes and compare it to the highlight. Which is lightest? The one rule of reflected light is that it can never be as light as the main light (**2B**).

Before you start painting a subject, whether from a photo or from life, ask yourself where the light is coming from (look for cast shadows to give you clues). Look through the projects in this book and try to guess the direction of the light in each painting.

2A

2B

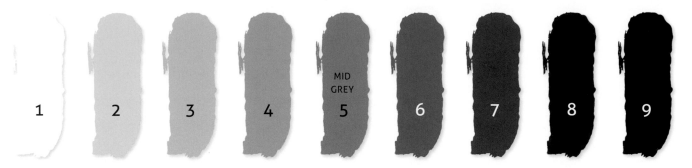

| 1 | 2 | 3 | 4 | MID GREY 5 | 6 | 7 | 8 | 9 |

The tonal scale from white to black.

3A

3B

Tonal scale

Judging the steps between black and white is so important that we sometimes use a tonal scale to help us. The scale has an odd number of steps so that we have a middle-value grey. In the first project we will be mixing values 1 to 5 of the 9-value scale. You may wish to create the full scale as an exercise in mixing accurate tonal values.

Tonal pattern

The success of a painting lies not only in achieving an accurate depiction of the subject. Most successful compositions (apart from the work of pure colourists) are based on a simple arrangement of light and dark shapes. This doesn't happen by chance. Artists deliberately select and adjust their subjects to achieve a simple pattern of tonal values.

Squinting at your subject (or a painting) reduces the amount of distracting detail and enables you to identify the pattern of lights and darks. Squinting at this finished painting (**3A**) will reveal a tonal pattern like the image below (**3B**). Note how, even in a complex subject, the light and dark shapes are grouped together into a relatively simple pattern.

Single colour swatch

Colour Theory

Colour is the most mysterious and wonderful aspect of painting. People respond to colours in an emotional way, but as painters we are privileged to observe and work with them on a deeper level. Basic colour theory is the ideal place to start our journey into the absorbing world of colour.

It's possible to think that learning colour theory will hinder your ability to use colour instinctively. My suggestion is that you absorb every theory you can in order to learn how colours behave, yet reserve the right to use any colour you like just because you feel like it.

In a painting, no colour is seen in isolation. Dark surroundings make colours appear lighter, while dull neighbours make some more vibrant.

Colour qualities

Any colour can be accurately described using just three attributes: colour, tonal value and intensity. Let's describe the swatch shown above by these qualities.

1. Starting with the most obvious quality, the colour, we can say it's a blue. Now look at the colour wheel (see opposite page, top right) and ask yourself, which way does the blue lean? Is it a greeny blue or a purple blue?

2. Now look at the tonal value. This is lightness or darkness, sometimes referred to as tone or simply value. If you were to take a black and white photo of a colour, you would see its tonal value. Choose a number from 1 to 9 on the value scale (see page 17) to match the tonal value.

3. Now consider the intensity. This is the quality of colour described by many different names (including chroma, power, saturation and depth), but they all mean the strength or purity of the colour. Is the colour intense or dull?

Normally, colours straight from the tube are at their most intense. As they get mixed with white, black or other (especially complementary) colours, they become duller. I would say it's a purply blue, with a tonal value around 5 and its intensity is dull.

Primary and secondary colours

In theory, we can mix all the colours in the rainbow from the three primaries: red, yellow and blue. In practice, I would say we could mix 85 per cent of colours. By adding a red, so that we have a warm and a cool variety, I would say that jumps to 95 per cent.

Secondary colours (green, purple and orange) can be mixed from primary colours. I couldn't resist adding a tube of a secondary colour (viridian) to our list because it makes mixing greens easier and without it we couldn't get my favourite colour – turquoise.

Complementary colours

Exploring colour

COLOUR WHEEL MIXES

If you've never done one before, it's
a good idea to make a colour wheel
from your actual colours so that you
understand how they relate to each
other. Start by laying out your tubes in
a circle so that you can visualize where
they sit. Make sure your cool red (alizarin
crimson) sits next to blue and your
warm red (cadmium) sits next to yellow.
A 12-segment wheel is easy to draw,
starting with a cross through the circle.
Begin with the primary colours, placed
three spaces apart. We have yellow and
blue, but no primary red, so mix your
two reds to fill the primary red slot.

Some colours (phthalo blue/viridian)
appear almost black from the tube. Add
a little white to these so that you can see
their character clearly.

HARMONIOUS COLOURS

Harmonious colours get on really well
together. They sit close to each other on
the colour wheel and when combined in
a painting, there's never any fighting.

WARM AND COOL COLOURS

On the colour wheel, there is a warm,
orange side (like the colours of fire) and
a cool, blue side (like ice.) Then there
are the in-between colours which can
be either warm or cool. Any colour
that seems orangey is warm, while
one which leans towards blue is cool.

COMPLEMENTARY COLOURS

Complementary colours are the odd
couples of the colour wheel – direct
opposites, such as red and green, blue
and orange, yellow and purple. Like
strong personalities, put them side by
side and by their difference they make
each other shine. Mix them together
and they kill each other.

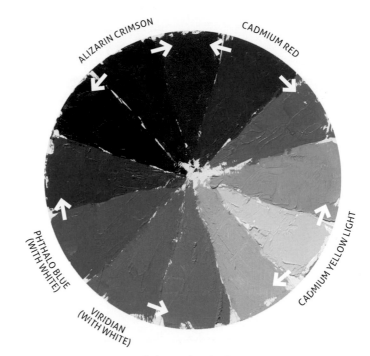

Colour wheel mixes

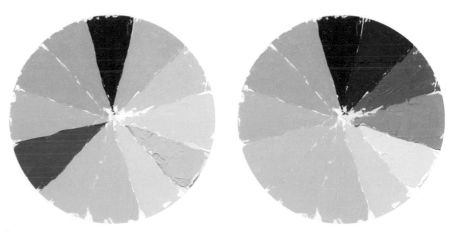

A primary colour wheel   *Harmonious colours*

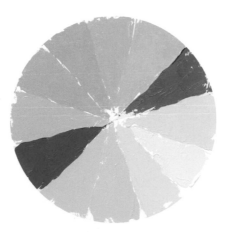

Complementary colour wheel

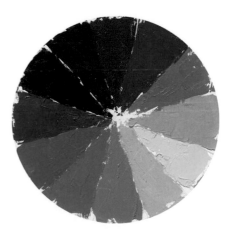

Warm and cool colours

THREE COLOUR SCHEMES

LEFT *This is a riot of colour for me. I was helped by working over a previous painting that had been abandoned by my wife. Allowing some of the original colours to show through broke me out of my own habitual colours.*

BELOW *A scheme based on orange/ blue complementary colours. Everything is suffused in a dim blue light in order for the furnace to appear stronger.*

RIGHT *The challenge here was to do an entire painting using leftover piles of 'palette mud'. Despite having no strong colours, the reddest colours appear stronger because they are surrounded by dull greenish ones.*

LAYOUT OF THE PALETTE

Squeeze paints out around the edge of your palette, leaving the maximum area for mixing in the centre. Set them out in a logical order, and use the same order each time you paint. You don't want to have to search for the right colour.

My palette (see right) is divided into two colour wheels. On the left is the Chromatic colour wheel of five colours. These are the fun, children's paintbox type colours. On the right is the Earth colour wheel, consisting of just three colours. Think of them as duller versions of the chromatic colours. Black is earth blue, burnt sienna is earth orange and yellow ochre is, you guessed it, earth yellow. They are not entirely necessary as they could be created from the chromatic colours, but they do save us time when mixing.

The layout of my palette.

Always put out at least three blobs of white in the central mixing area. We use more white than anything else and we need separate blobs to mix with different colours. To give yourself a full range of colours, mix some nice clean secondary colours before you start. Use the palette knife to mix a purple from blue and crimson and an orange from cadmium red and yellow. If you are painting a landscape with bright greens, you may also want a yellow-green. If you wait till you are in the middle of the painting before mixing these colours, they are likely to get muddied.

WHEN PAINTING WITH COLOUR

Daylight is the best light for painting in as it contains all the wavelengths of light and gives full colour. Rarely can you get perfect light on the subject, the canvas and your palette, but aim for it anyway. You should almost never use colour straight from the tube without modifying it. When you need to mix colour, bear in mind that the strongest mixes come from colours which are close together on the colour wheel. For your best purple, use cool red (crimson) and blue.

Pure white and pure black are colourless. Always add something to keep them interesting. Blacks can be varied by adding crimson, blue or burnt sienna. Or make your own blacks from brown and blue or crimson and viridian.

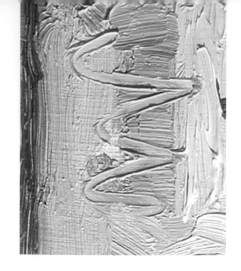

Painting Techniques

Every artist builds a personal repertoire of marks which they naturally use as they work. Here are some of mine. Experiment to see which suit you and which don't. Look at the techniques and tools used by other artists, invent your own and you will develop an armoury of marks to tackle any subject.

When using oils, there are no right or wrong brushmarks. A technique may be used to imitate the texture of the subject, but it doesn't have to. We are not painting a door; your strokes don't need to be neat or parallel. Remember, you can't mix colour accurately or make luscious marks with a meagre amount of paint. Squeeze out twice as much as you think you need – and use it all!

Diluting paint

For most of the painting, the consistency of paint that comes out of the tube is perfect. Don't leave your brushes bristles-down in a jar of solvent (as you might do when working with acrylics) because your mixtures will be too sloppy. However, there are times when you will want the paint to flow more readily, for ease of drawing or to apply thin washes.

In your first session on a painting, just use solvent if you need to dilute the paint. For all except one of the projects in this book, that is all you will need.

THIN WASH (MESSY)
This can be used to tone the whole canvas before you start, or for 'blocking in' various colours. Dip the tip of your brush into solvent and make a pool on your palette. Now dip into some paint and mix this into the pool. Apply the wash in all directions (**1**).

THIN WASH (WIPED SMOOTH)
Use a rag to gently wipe the thin wash for a more even coverage (**2**).

Painting wet-in-wet

Most of the paintings in this book are done 'alla prima', which means in one go. They are completed in anything between one and a half to four hours. To complete a painting in this way, we need to be able to paint 'wet-in-wet', laying wet paint on top of an already wet surface (**3**). Whether you are using

the brush or the knife, to make a mark that does not get mixed in with under-lying paint, you will need: a well-loaded brush (or knife) of non-diluted paint, a light touch and a single, decisive stroke.

Decide where you're going to put the stroke, do it in one go and leave it. The mark will never be perfect, but it will look confident and exciting. Repeated corrections will muddy the effect. If it's really not an acceptable mark, wipe it off and re-do it. Before doing the next stroke, wipe off the brush on a rag and re-insert it in a clean pile

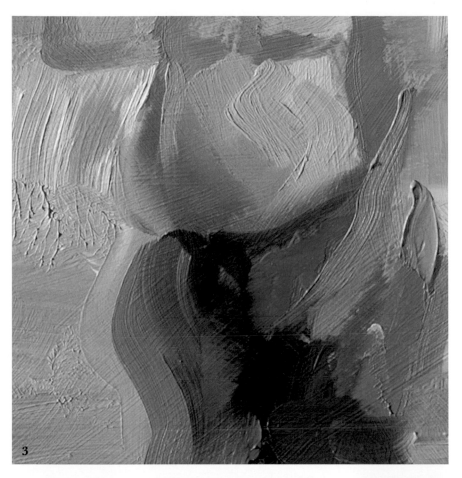

3

of paint. One teacher told me that a paintbrush is a rifle that needs to be reloaded each time you fire, not a machine gun to be fired repeatedly.

IMPASTO WET-IN-WET

Undiluted thick paint is known as 'impasto' (Italian for 'paste'). The thicker it gets, the more messy and exciting it is to paint into! (**4**).

LIFT-OFF TECHNIQUE

Dip a brush into a large pile of paint. When you lift the brush out, a peak of paint will appear at the tip. Placed gently on your painting, this makes a deliciously sharp highlight (**5**).

'Always use a full brush and a larger one than necessary.'

John Singer Sargent

4

5

Starting to paint

You will always need more time at the
end, so don't aim for perfection at the
start. Get the canvas covered as soon as
you can, leaving time to correct later.
As you start painting, pick up a clean
brush for each new mixture. Using lots
of brushes (I used at least twelve) keeps
your colours separate and clean.

Remember, it's impossible to
mix clean colours on a dirty palette.
As soon as you are struggling to find
a clean patch, wipe it off and refresh
any depleted piles of paint.

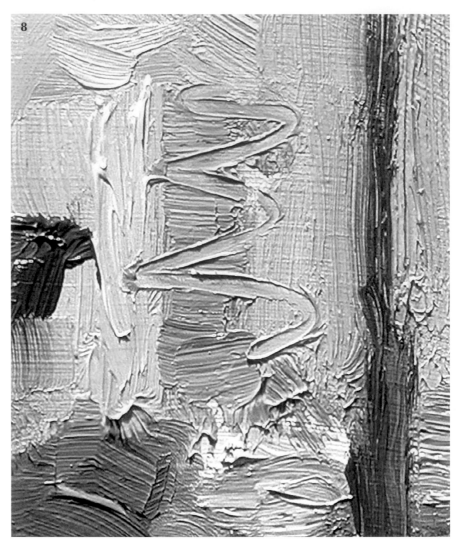

Removing paint

When painting wet-in-wet, most
corrections can be made by applying
the new colour directly on top. However,
drastic changes (such as from a very
light colour to a dark one) work best if
you remove some paint first. The palette
knife, rag and telephone directory are
all ideal for removing paint, sometimes
resulting in exciting textures, which can
be left in the final painting.

PALETTE KNIFE

Use a palette knife for controlled
removal of excess paint. It often reveals
more exciting textures than you could
create deliberately (**6**).

TONKING

Named after the British painter Henry
Tonks, this technique aims to reduce
the amount of paint on the surface
without smudging the image. You just
need to place a piece of absorbent paper
onto the surface and peel it off. Just
think, some day they could name
a painting technique after you (**7**)!

SGRAFFITO

The Italian word for 'scratched' is used
for the technique of removing paint
with the wrong end of the brush or the
tip of a palette knife. Lines scratched
through wet paint sometimes reveal
underlying colours. This technique can
also be used to sign your painting (**8**).

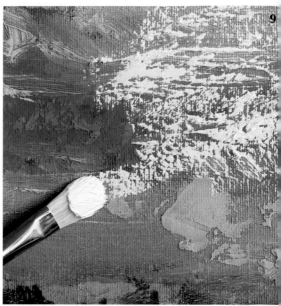

Textures with brush and knife

With hog-hair brushes and a palette knife, you can create hundreds of paint textures. While some work best wet-in-wet, others make use of dried paint layers.

SCUMBLE
Undiluted paint dragged over a rough, dry surface is called a scumble. Hold the brush gently at the angle shown so that the paint only catches on the top ridges of the underlying layer (**9**).

SCUMBLE EFFECT USING KNIFE
Undiluted paint on the back of the knife can be rubbed over a rough surface for a similar effect to the scumble (**10**).

KNIFE STAMP
To create straight lines, stamp the edge of the painting knife in paint and place it on the canvas (**11**).

KNIFE STRIATIONS
Put various colours into a pile of paint but don't mix them. When applied to the canvas with the knife, the striations of colour give a spectacular effect (**12**).

Softening paint

Most of the brushmarks we make have hard edges. Here are three of my favourite ways of softening things down to make subtle colour transitions.

TORN TOWEL

Use a torn piece of kitchen paper. Dragged gently through thick paint, the edges are softened in a lively way (**13**).

FINGER PAINTING

You can, of course, paint with your fingers, but more frequently I use them to create really soft or 'lost' edges (**14**).

SQUEEGEE SMUDGING

A piece of card, a plank of wood, almost anything with a flat edge can be dragged across the entire painting to smudge and remove paint. It's surprising how good the painting can look after this drastic move (**15**)!

Adding linseed oil

If you return to a painting after the first layer has dried, just add a little linseed oil to your solvent for whenever you wish to dilute the paint. This mixture of solvent and linseed oil is called a medium. (Two parts solvent to one part linseed oil is a reliable recipe.) In doing this, you are following the 'fat over lean' rule. The top layers of your painting will contain more oil (fat) and dry more slowly, meaning there is no danger of it cracking as it dries. (The same principle applies when painting oils over acrylics, which is alright because the oils dry more slowly. However, painting acrylics over oils is not recommended.)

Glazing

We use the same medium (solvent and linseed oil) to make a glaze. Check that the first layer of paint is completely dry,

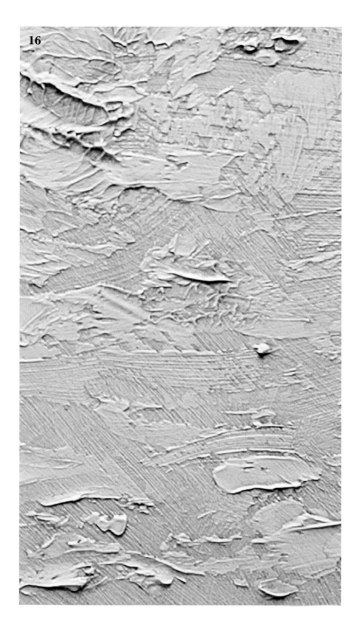

16

17

then mix your painting medium with any combination of transparent paints and you have a glaze. When applied, the effect is to change the colour of the underlying layer without losing detail.

Glazing is a technique you can easily do without – and many artists do. I'm including it here because it creates effects of transparent colour, which aren't possible through direct painting.

When selecting colours for glazing, it's important to check that they are transparent rather than opaque. Most (not all) paint tubes will tell you. Winsor & Newton use symbols on their tubes

to indicate transparency. If in doubt, check the manufacturer's paint charts. Colours that are good for glazing are permanent alizarin crimson, phthalo blue, viridian hue and burnt sienna.

The technique of mixing a glaze is exactly the same as that used for making a thin wash (see page 22). The only difference is that medium is used instead of pure solvent and only transparent paints are used. Once applied, you may leave the glaze as it is or wipe it with a rag to adjust the darkness (more wiping leads to a lighter colour). Glazing will rarely be the final

step in a painting. You can paint on top of a glaze immediately with any technique you like.

A glaze can be used to emphasize the texture of impasto brushmarks. After applying the glaze, gently wipe the top ridges with a rag, leaving paint in the hollows. This is a classic Rembrandt technique (**16**).

A velatura (meaning 'veil') is a glaze that incorporates white or opaque colours, resulting in a milky appearance. It is often used over distant mountains to help make them recede or to create realistic clouds (**17**).

Teacup

In this project you will learn to mix a range of tonal values and use them to convey light and shade on a white object. Working in black and white helps you to master tone without being distracted by colour.

COLOURS NEEDED

Ivory
Black

Titanium
White

When you love colour as much as I do, it's tempting to skip over tonal value and head for the exciting stuff. Only when you buckle down and start to look carefully at a white object do you see the true beauty and subtlety that is there. If you can nail the ability to see lights and darks, you can use the craziest colour in the world and get away with it.

You can copy my painting of a teacup or do your own painting of any simple white object. Place your object on a white surface and make sure it is lit by one main light source from the side, such as window or a lamp. Position your canvas level with the subject so that you can compare them at a glance.

PRE-MIXING COLOURS

To give yourself a head start, it's a good idea to mix a few tonal values ready to drop into the painting. To paint a white object, we will only need five values (white to middle grey) and we already have white, so it won't take long. For pre-mixing colours, I encourage you to use a palette knife to gain some practice in handling this tool. The knife is very easy to clean off between mixes, meaning that you don't get bits of one colour mixed into another by mistake.

Start by squeezing out white paint for tonal value 1 in the lower left of your palette, followed by black and at least three blobs of white for mixing the rest of the greys. Mix middle grey (tonal value 5) first, comparing your mixture with black and white until it sits equally between them (you will use more white paint than black). Next mix tonal value 3, to sit equally between values 1 and 5, and finally values 2 and 4.

The setup for your work. If you are right-handed, it's preferable to have the easel to your right (so that you are not reaching across yourself) and your subject on the left.

Mix tonal values 1–5. Check that you have fairly even steps between them and adjust if need be.

STAGE 1

There are two good reasons for using a light colour for the initial drawing. Firstly, it gives us chance to get it wrong. We can easily mix up a darker colour and redraw on top. Secondly, let's imagine we did our drawing in black. Every light colour we put on top will mix with the black and get muddy.

Dilute tonal value 2 to make the paint flow easily and use a No. 2 round brush to draw the shapes on your canvas. Make the shape of the object fill the square as much as possible. Outline the shape of the shadows too – they connect the object to the edges of the picture.

To make the inevitable corrections your drawing will need, use kitchen towel dipped in solvent as an eraser. If you feel like checking proportions, try to find something vertical which matches something horizontal in the picture. Here the height of the cup is equal to the distance from the left side of the cup to the middle of the handle. It's not critical at this stage, but if you want to check if your ellipse is symmetrical, look at it in the mirror.

Tip

Before you start, swing the brush around just above the surface of the canvas. Feel your confidence – you are in control of the whole painting. If you feel like it, splodge some paint anywhere on the canvas just to show who is in charge!

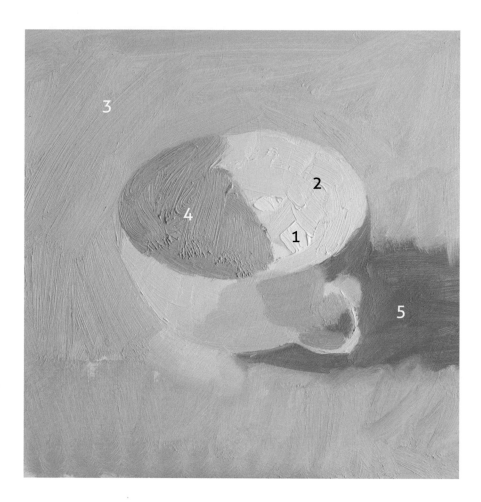

STAGE 2

The next step is to identify the very lightest thing in your subject. When looking for tonal values, try squinting. Almost close your eyes and notice how all the complexity of the subject is reduced to simple areas of light and dark. Here the lightest things are the highlights in the cup, reflecting the window. Blob in some thick white paint, just as a marker and reminder that everything in the whole canvas must be made darker than these notes in order for them to sing (**1**).

Now look for the very darkest parts of the subject, areas which are around value 5. Think only in terms of shapes, not objects. Note how I have painted across the edge of the cup, grouping the cast shadow and the dark side of the cup together into one shape.

Now that you have marked the lightest and darkest areas, you can work in any order, blocking in big shapes with one of your five tonal values. Many beginners ask what to do first. Is it darks before lights, or background before subject? The real answer is that you can do it in any order you please. In practice, I look at the painting, then at the subject and ask myself, what's one big thing I can do to make the painting more like the subject? That's what I do next.

Tip

Use your finger to soften the hard edges of the block-in stage. I like to use the side of my little finger because it is smaller than my forefinger. It also seems appropriate to use your extended pinky for the delicate job of painting a teacup!

STAGE 3

To keep the viewer interested in a painting, aim for variety in many aspects of the painting. This includes the thickness of the paint. As a general rule, aim for thin darks and thick lights. This is because thick paint sticks out and catches the light, an advantage with light colours because it makes them appear lighter. In darker passages, we generally don't want too many ridges of paint because the light will catch on them and disrupt the effect of darkness. At this stage the thick paint in the shadowy interior of the cup was distracting, so I used the palette knife to scrape it off.

We noted earlier that every colour is affected by surrounding colours. While there is still some white unpainted board peeping through, we cannot truly judge all the tonal values. Now that the white is covered, we can see where we stand and make finer adjustments in tonal value. One such area is the shadow inside the cup, where one block of tone has been made into two.

STAGE 4

You could stop at the previous stage but for me, the cup just didn't feel very special, so I took a piece of torn kitchen towel and dragged it through the thick areas of paint, breaking the hard edges. I also used the palette knife, scraping paint off and moving it around to create more texture. If you are brave enough to soften all the edges in this way, each new brushmark will appear crisp and sharp.

I introduced the table edge because of the big empty space on the left and the sense that the cup was floating in mid-air. Swirly marks with the No. 4 bristle brush give a sense of cloth over the table. If you want your brushmarks in the final painting to have texture and swing, keep using large bristle brushes until the end. My smallest brush was reserved for the signature and the delicate cross in the highlight that indicates the window frame.

Break up hard edges by dragging torn kitchen towel through the paint.

The lighter parts of the cup were painted with softer synthetic brushes and the highlights laid on gently after using the lift-off technique (see page 23) to get a nice glob of paint.

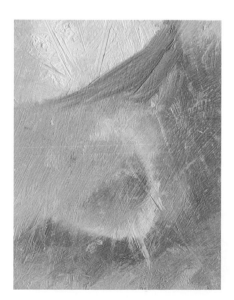

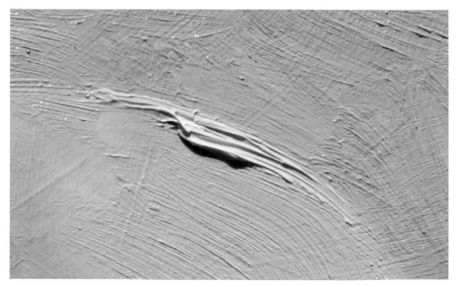

FOCUS ON
Composition

When you first start painting, it is enough to try to get some resemblance of the subject. Soon, however, you will feel the urge to move some element of the subject or omit it entirely. This is your natural sense of composition speaking and you should listen. Composition is simply the way things are arranged in a rectangle.

'Rules' of composition

Good compositions arise from a willingness to change things until they look right. Having said that, a few ideas about what to look for (or avoid) can help you if you get stuck. Like all rules in painting, they are there to be learned, understood and broken at will. Doing lots of small drawings of good paintings is the best education in how to put a painting together. Always include the borders of the rectangle (**1**).

FOCAL POINT
Just like a play, a painting needs lead characters and a supporting cast. If everyone has a lead role, there is chaos. Try to decide what you want the viewer to notice first in your painting and which elements you will keep subdued.

Things that catch the eye are detail and texture, contrasts of dark and light and contrasts of colour, hard edges, strong colours and people.

In this painting of Watermouth Harbour and Castle (**2**) the focal point is created by the contrast of the two strongest complementary colours, orange and blue, which have been put right next to each other.

DON'T WANDER OFF
Let's keep them interested. Unbroken horizontal lines can lead the viewer out of the painting. Well-placed verticals can stop them wandering off. The wine bottle and table leg perform this role in 'Writer's Block' (compare the right-hand sides of **3A** and **3B**).

4

Viewfinder

One of the most useful tools to help you compose is the viewfinder. Especially when faced with an overwhelming subject, a simple piece of card with a hole in it can help you select a view and envision the arrangement of your finished picture. The proportions of the aperture (hole) should match your canvas. For a 10 x 12in (25 x 30cm) canvas, you should cut an aperture of 6 x 5in (12 x 10cm).

When you are happy with what you see through the viewfinder, you can translate that exact arrangement onto your canvas. Mark half and quarter ways on the inside edge of the viewfinder, as well as the outside edges of your canvas. Holding the viewfinder in position, note any part of the subject that coincides with (or comes close to) one of your edge marks. Now mark the position of that element on your canvas.

Use your first few marks as 'anchor points' to help you return the viewfinder to the same position. Once you have 8–10 marks on your canvas, you can connect up the drawing knowing that everything is in the right place (**6**).

DIAGONALS

Diagonals indicate movement and I love to incorporate them whenever possible. Like everything else, they need to be balanced. Lots of diagonals going one way will make the viewer feel like they are tilting. In the picture above, the upward sloping shadow in the lower left was introduced to balance a generally downward sloping composition (**4**).

RULE OF THIRDS

Lines which divide the rectangle equally down the middle (vertically or horizontally) leave the viewer not sure which half to look at. We are much more at ease with paintings divided into thirds (see bottom left). A focal point can also look better on a junction of thirds than bang in the centre (**5**).

5

6

Kitchen Still Life

*Still life is a great subject in its own right, but it is also ideal training ground
for more challenging subjects. The skills you learn in this project (composing your
shapes, creating light and shade and mixing colours) will all be essential when
you are faced with more fleeting subjects later on.*

COLOURS NEEDED

Phthalo
Blue

Viridian
Hue

Cadmium
Yellow
Pale

Yellow
Ochre

Burnt
Sienna

Permanent
Alizarin
Crimson

Cadmium
Red

Ivory
Black

Titanium
White

COMPOSING YOUR STILL LIFE

There are two things to consider when choosing objects to paint in a still life. Firstly, their shapes and colours should look good together. Look for simple, undecorated objects, not all the same size. The second thing is the theme: the story the objects will tell in the finished painting.

You may copy my painting if you wish, or compose your own still life of any three objects. The simple act of playing around with objects, swapping them around, moving them back and forth, develops your ability to compose.

As you arrange your objects, try varying the angles of the handles and overlapping your objects slightly to connect them together. Notice how different your subject looks from different viewpoints – seated or standing. As in the previous project, use a single light source from one side to give the objects a light side and a dark side. You may use a viewfinder (see page 35) to view the setup, moving the objects around until you are happy with the arrangement.

Looking through the viewfinder at my subject helped me to see that the area in the top right was empty and that the horizontal edge of the table led straight out of the picture. I used a piece of card to cast an arrow-shaped shadow into this area, directing our attention back into the picture where it belongs.

Everything contributes to the composition, including the arrangement of colours. I have chosen objects in complementary colours – orange and blue. For variety, I introduced some lime green into the background. The orange mug looked a bit isolated, so I placed an orange shopping bag to the left of the objects. This reflects some orange into the teapot and milk jug.

Tip
Painting objects under a constant light source gives you time to work towards a realistic result in three easy stages. Start by blocking in the local (basic) colour of each object. Then develop the effect of light and shade (one side lighter, the other darker) and finally note the way colours reflect from one surface to another.

STAGE 1

The first job is drawing the position of the objects on the canvas. This is done with diluted yellow, which is easy to correct or paint over. Once you have the rough positions outlined, do a more accurate drawing on top, using different colours to distinguish it from the first drawing. You don't want these lines to muddy what you put on top, so use diluted blue for the teapot and orange for everything else.

STAGE 2

Now you need to block in the local (basic) colours of the objects. As colours mix together in the process of painting, they naturally get duller, so it makes sense to start slightly stronger than you eventually need. It's also much easier to subdue a colour than to make it more intense.

Yellow is one of the most easily contaminated colours, so let's start with the background yellow-greens. In the final painting we can make them darker and greener, but at this stage use pure yellow with a touch of viridian. Work around all the blocks of colour, diluting the paint slightly to make it cover more quickly. Within minutes, you will have achieved a strong effect with flat shapes of colour.

Some artists are adept at designing complete pictures with flat shapes. If this comes naturally to you, you may have found your style already!

STAGE 3

Just because we are working in colour does not mean that the lessons of tonal value go out the window. Here we do exactly the same thing we did with the previous painting. Identify the lightest part of the scene (the rim of the milk jug) by squinting. Mark that with pure white, put on with the palette knife, and tell yourself that nothing must compete with that for whiteness. Even things we know to be white, such as the inside of the orange mug, cannot be pure white.

It can be more difficult to see differences in tonal value when we are looking at brightly coloured objects. One trick is to look at the subject reflected in the black screen of your smartphone or tablet. Like squinting, this makes everything darker, but it also reduces the confusing effect of strong colours.

Here, I tried to create light and shade by adding white to the light side and black to the shadow side. It's not bad, but neither white nor black have any colour in them, so the mug loses some of its intensity.

To make objects look three-dimensional, you need to create a light side and a dark side. The challenge is to do this without entirely losing the strong local colours we established in the previous stage. A simple approach to creating a light side can be seen in the orange mug and milk jug. Use a rag to gently wipe the light side of the objects. Where the paint is thinner, it appears lighter. The blue teapot has been developed further. Rather than just using black and white, use varied patches of colour to create lights and darks while maintaining colour interest.

STAGE 4

For the shadow side of the mug, you need dark colours, which are also intensely orange. A mixture of crimson and burnt sienna does the trick.

Combining local colour with the effects of light and shade certainly gives a realistic look but there is another level of observation you could add to the visual excitement. The arrows indicate where the colour of one thing is reflected in another. The lime green wall reflects into the teapot and the white groundsheet takes on some of the colour of the mug and wall. Most people never even notice these subtle, beautiful effects, but you are an artist, so you will start to see them everywhere.

Tip
As well as creating more interesting colour, reflected colours tie all the objects together and make them look like they are sitting in the same space.

STAGE 5

This final stage involves softening some edges with the finger and adding the highlights. Like cherries on a cake, one or two highlights are a treat, but don't get carried away. Put them on confidently and don't fiddle. If a highlight really doesn't work out, it's better to wipe it off entirely and redo it.

Highlights should be distinct enough to sing, but also need to remain connected to the surface they are sitting on. The highlights on the blue teapot contain a touch of purple, while those on the orange mug contain a hint of crimson to keep them connected to the object. Softening some edges of the larger highlights is another way to prevent them looking stuck on. The example of the mug on page 39 shows some over-enthusiastic highlighting.

And now for the final flourish. Your signature is an important part of the painting. Sign with the materials you are using in the painting – that way it is much more difficult to forge! An ostentatious signature can distract from the artwork itself. You should be able to see it if you're looking for it, but it shouldn't scream at you. Artists tend to sign their work in the lower right or left corners. I look for a corner that looks a bit empty or badly painted. That way, the viewer will see the signature and not the poor work underneath! Your signature can also be a last chance to balance your painting. Here I felt that there was blue in most areas of the painting, but not in the lower right, so that is where it landed.

Master Copy

All great artists of the past learned by copying the work of those they admired. To learn about composition, copy the whole painting. If it is the brushmarks or the way the artist has painted particular objects that inspires you, copy a 'detail' (small section) of the original.

COLOURS NEEDED

| Phthalo Blue | Viridian Hue | Cadmium Yellow Pale | Yellow Ochre | Burnt Sienna | Permanent Alizarin Crimson | Cadmium Red | Ivory Black | Titanium White |

The Great Walnut Tree, *Pontoise, 1875,*
Camille Pissarro (1830–1903)

It's fun to become your chosen artist for an
hour or two and imagine what it was like to
paint the original masterpiece. I love Pissarro
for his honesty in front of nature. His colours
are true, his brushwork unfussy. You don't need
to know what it is you like about your chosen
painting before you start – you will discover
that as you go along. You may wish to copy
the Pissarro I have chosen, but I think you will
learn more by copying a painting that excites
you personally, particularly if you can see the
original masterwork with the actual colours and
brushstrokes used.

CROPPING AND GRIDDING THE BOARD

It's important to crop your painting board to
match the proportions of the original painting.
If you are working from a photo without borders,
just place it in the corner of your board and lay
a ruler through the corners. Where this line
intersects the edge of the board is where it needs
to be cropped to match the proportions of the
original painting (**1**).

If your photo has white borders, is in a book
or on a screen, place a thin piece of paper (or
tracing paper) over the image, aligning two

edges of the paper with one corner of the image.
Make a dot where the opposite corner of the
image is (**2**). The paper can then be placed in
the corner of your board and a ruler located
diagonally from the corner, through the dot,
until it meets the edge of the board, marking
where it needs to be cropped. Use a craft knife
to crop the board and watch your fingers (**3**).

Now that the proportions are the same,
you have the option of gridding up the original
to make the drawing easier. Simply divide
the image into halves and quarters. The same
divisions drawn on your canvas (or even just
corresponding marks around the edges) make
the placing of the major lines much easier.

Tip

Try to find out the
dimensions of the
original painting,
otherwise you could
find yourself trying
to copy a huge
painting onto a tiny
canvas, wondering
why you can't get
the same level
of detail as the
original. Of course,
there is no reason
why you can't make
a small copy of
a large painting,
but yours will be a
simplified version.

STAGE 1

Look carefully at your chosen original and see if you can identify any of the ground colour peeping through (this is much easier from actual paintings). For this piece, Pissarro worked over a textured ground, possibly even a previous painting. The few underlayers that peep through, around the branches of the trees, appear to be beige, so I chose a board primed with leftover oil paint to something like this colour. The oil priming gives the surface a little more roughness.

Using a grid over the original and related marks around the edges of your canvas to guide you, do a reasonably careful drawing with a No. 2 round brush and diluted paint. Then, starting with the lightest colour, paint the building with white and a touch of orange. To another pile of white, add a touch of blue and apply this roughly to the sky. The scattered clouds are made with white and a touch of cadmium red, to almost the same tonal value as the sky itself. Having noted the lightest colours, look for the darkest to give the full tonal range. These darks are not pure black but have blue, crimson and white mixed in.

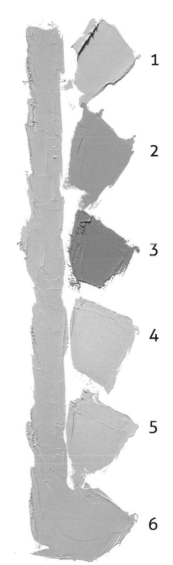

Tip
You will arrive at the right colour by asking yourself three questions: should it be lighter or darker, what colour does it need more of and should it be duller or more intense? Complementary colours are useful for quickly dulling each other.

STAGE 2

In copying a painting, the problems of drawing and composition are all solved. The challenge lies in matching the artist's colours. You don't need any special training to achieve an exact colour match and there is never just one way to arrive at the right colour. I will take you through my process in matching the colour of the path in Pissarro's painting. It may seem slow at first, but you will get much quicker with practice.

Start with white and add some blue (**1**). Add more blue until the tonal value is about right (**2**). Now it is too intense (too blue). Add some orange (complementary of blue) to kill the colour (**3**). Now it is too dark and too green.

Add lots of white to lighten the colour (**4**).

Red is the complement of green, so add touches of both red and crimson to kill the green. Because these make the colour darker, also add white to bring it back to the correct tonal value (**5**).

Now for the final step. The colour needs to be slightly darker and warmer, so we use burnt sienna. Picking up a blob of paint on the knife risks taking it too far, so use the knife to drag a stain of paint towards the centre of the palette. Add this gradually until you arrive at the perfect match (**6**).

Creating the colour for the path.

STAGE 3

Pissarro's painting is a lesson in creating a variety of greens. If we were to match each one individually, you can imagine how long it would take. A quicker approach is to mix generous piles of the most common greens with the palette knife and block these in to cover as much ground as possible. Then adjust the colours as necessary to match the variety in the painting.

Large piles of dark blue-green, medium green and light yellow-green used as the starting point for all the greens in the painting.

STAGE 4

The process of this painting involves mixing and applying large blocks of clean colour. It is only at this final stage that the finer lines, such as the branches and little commas of paint for the leaves, are applied. The original painting, at 16in (40cm) wide, is not significantly larger than my 12in (30cm) canvas. This means my brushstrokes can be fairly close to the size of those in the original.

Don't try to copy the exact shape of every brushmark, especially on an Impressionist painting. It is much quicker and simpler to emulate the spirit in which the marks were made. Imagine Pissarro on that dusty Pontoise road, jabbing his canvas excitedly to capture the last remnants of light.

FOCUS ON
Painting Outdoors

How often have you photographed a breathtaking scene, only to find on looking at the photo afterwards that it captured nothing of what you saw and felt in the moment? That's why, in spite of the myriad challenges involved, painters happily pack up their paints and go outdoors. They also know that there is an authenticity and liveliness to painting done on the spot, which is very difficult to replicate in the studio.

Outdoor painting became popular in France in the 19th century, helped by the availability of paint in tubes and the railway to take people to interesting locations. Hence we use a French term, 'en plein air', to describe the practice of painting outside.

Painting outdoors is the key to doing better paintings in half the time. The simple switch from cosy studio and static subject to the great outdoors, with its constantly changing sights and sounds, forces you to work quickly and simplify. Besides which, it's much more fun!

I'm not suggesting that you take your shiny new oil paints out into a field to do your very first oil painting. Play around first in the comfort of your home or studio. Get a few half-decent paintings under your belt to build your confidence, then get outdoors.

The first step is the hardest. It helps if you can find like-minded artists to go with when you first venture outdoors. Or you may ease into it by taking a few excursions with a sketchbook. That way, you won't be conspicuous, but you will begin investigating a subject face-to-face and you'll soon be hooked.

There are obvious challenges to painting outdoors. Here are some practical tips to keep you on track.

Outdoor Painting Materials

1. Primed boards of various colours
2. Backpack
3. Plastic bags for dirty rags
4. Tripod for pochade box
5. Kitchen towel
6. Pochade box (contains palette)
7. Baseball cap
8. Paints (obviously)
9. Dipper with lid
10. Low-odour solvent
11. Medium (2 parts solvent, 1 part linseed oil)
12. Palette knife
13. Old telephone directory
14. Mirror
15. Brushes and jar

Practical tips

Learn to pack just what you need. This takes trial and error, so expect a few kinks for the first two trips.

At the risk of sounding like your mother, wrap up warm and wear sensible shoes or a hat and sunscreen, whatever is applicable. You are going to be in one spot for some time. You may need a baseball cap to keep the sun out of your eyes. Don't spend too long when choosing a subject – the perfect one is not just around the corner. When faced with an overwhelming subject, the viewfinder can be helpful in isolating a view.

You can paint in any weather, but if possible keep yourself and your painting out of the wind, rain and direct sunshine – in that order. Wind is the worst. Flying materials are not easy to paint with. Rain is OK. It won't dissolve oil paint, but if you can find a sheltered spot, why not? Direct sunshine is lovely, but when it shines on your palette and painting, it makes it hard to judge colours. In compensating for the bright light, you may end up with a painting which is too dark.

Intrigued onlookers may wish to engage you in deep conversation about their aunt who paints. I find that polite but boring answers encourage them to move on to more interesting targets.

Expect the unexpected. Yes, a van may park right in front of you. Cows may appear from nowhere. Keep your sense of humour – it's only a painting.

Plein-air paintings can be an end in themselves or used as studies for larger works in the studio. The quality of the work does not depend on sticking to one method, indoors or out, but it's good to experience the benefits of both.

Woolacombe Beach, Devon, UK.

Boats at Sundown

This project introduces you to a quick technique suitable for painting fleeting subjects outdoors. You will devise a simple tonal plan, then proceed directly from a cursory drawing into applying thick luscious paint. You will learn to use the effects of aerial perspective to create depth in your painting.

COLOURS NEEDED

| Phthalo Blue | Viridian Hue | Cadmium Yellow Pale | Yellow Ochre | Burnt Sienna | Permanent Alizarin Crimson | Cadmium Red | Ivory Black | Titanium White |

This painting of the boats at Preston Marina, just round the corner from my studio, was completed in the last hour and a half of daylight. Although the light changes quickly in the morning and evening, providing a time challenge for the outdoor painter, artists love these 'golden hours'. The low sun casts dramatic shadows and the light has a much warmer glow than in the middle of the day. You can see by comparing the finished painting to the photo how the camera struggles to capture the subtle beauty of such dramatic lighting situations.

This piece is painted 'contre jour', a French term meaning 'into the light'. The sun is in front of you and most of the subject is in shadow, with just touches of light at the edges. You can copy my painting as an introduction to working in this direct manner or work from your own photo of a similar subject.

TONAL PLAN

When working outdoors in changing light, it is easy to start changing the painting over and over as the light moves. This chasing game is fun but unlikely to produce a good composition. To feel in control, it is best to devise a tonal plan before starting. Some artists do thumbnail sketches to organize their tonal values. I find it quicker to eye up the subject through a viewfinder (see page 35), squinting to reduce it to a pattern of light and dark shapes similar to this blurred photo (see above right). Zoom the viewfinder in and out and try it both vertically and horizontally. The view you settle on is your tonal plan. Try to stick to this arrangement of lights and darks.

Trust your instincts. Go with what looks best to you at the time and you will often happen upon one of the compositional 'rules'. Here the lightest part of the scene, the reflection of the sun on the water, is bound to draw the eye, especially as it is right next to the darkest area of the harbour wall. I avoided putting this focal point in the middle of the painting, but found that it looked better around the lower-right third.

The overlay image.

STAGE 1

The excitement (or sometimes panic) of trying to capture a subject outdoors leads to changes in technique. Rather than a careful drawing followed by the blocking in of local colours, here you will execute a rapid drawing using a mixture of brown, black and white, very diluted to make the paint flow.

The important thing, and the reason I went to the trouble of marking half and quarter ways around the edges of the canvas, is that the large shapes are where I want them, relating to the view through the viewfinder.

It takes courage to proceed from such a cursory drawing directly into thick paint, but remember you can always correct things later. To prove it, I have overlaid my initial outlines onto an image of the finished painting. You can see the places where I haven't quite got the drawing right to start with.

The marks in a painting tell the whole story of how it is made. Armchair painting will not result in lively, energetic marks. In this project, I challenge you to start piling on the paint right from the start. The edgy feeling of correcting as you go lends an urgency to your marks that you can't achieve in any other way.

STAGE 2

To cover the canvas as soon as possible, use your largest brushes (No. 6 and 8) and start with the largest blocks of colour. The warm, delicate colours of the sky and water should be put down early so that they don't get muddied. The sky is a simple mix of yellow, red and white. Any colour reflected in water appears darker and duller, so add some viridian and crimson to this mix for the colour of the water.

Leave a slice of clean canvas in the sky (to be filled in later) and for the brightest reflection in the water. Notice how these areas glow once everything else is made a little darker. You can add to this impression of luminosity by creating a 'halo' of warm colours around the brightest areas. Have fun with the swirly strokes of orange around the sunlight on the water. Wherever the trees meet the sky, introduce more touches of orange and yellow.

A halo of warm colour conveys the power of the light to dissolve the edges of whatever it comes in contact with. The painting shows glowing light with a warm halo (above) and without (below). Which do you prefer?

STAGE 3

To make the reflection of the sun on the water catch as much light as possible, use the tip of the palette knife to deposit pure white paint into that area.

Returning to the sky, mix up a generous pile of light blue and fill in the white gap with a few bold strokes, resisting the urge to correct or blend. If you had painted the whole of the sky with orange-yellow and then brushed the blue section into it, the resulting mix would have been a dull green – not great for a glowing sky. As it is, the orange and blue sit side by side, complementing each other.

Even though you haven't been too meticulous with the perspective lines, you can still create a sense of depth in this scene through a wonderful effect called aerial perspective. Paint your darkest tonal values in the foreground, gradually getting lighter as you move into the distance. This mimics the layers of atmosphere, containing moisture and dust, which make distant things more hazy.

STAGE 4

You won't have time to paint every boat mast, but if you note the way they get thinner and their tops appear to get lower as they go into the distance, you can use them to add to the impression of distance. To make a mast, place the edge of the palette knife into a pile of pink/purple paint and stamp this onto the painting, sometimes dragging downwards. In accordance with perspective, the closest mast is darker and wider than the more distant ones.

As you can see, I'm no expert at painting boats, but I do love to paint light. Treat yourself to the highlight on the left-hand boat, but start with a large blob of orange-yellow to create a halo, followed by a smaller blob of white in the centre. There is just time for the warm (orange) reflected light on the underside of the hull and its reflection in the water.

Be careful if you find yourself having too much fun adding details – you must know when to stop. If your painting has captured your impression of the scene, the viewer can fill in the details. When it comes to your signature, if there is no obvious area that needs covering up, nor any colour that needs balancing, go for the unobtrusive option and scratch your name into the wet paint with the handle of your brush.

Cityscape

To paint the effect of morning light in the city, you will learn to mix warm light colours and cool darks. You will also create the illusion of receding space by learning the simple rules of perspective and applying them in your painting of buildings and figures.

COLOURS NEEDED

| Phthalo Blue | Viridian Hue | Cadmium Yellow Pale | Yellow Ochre | Burnt Sienna | Permanent Alizarin Crimson | Cadmium Red | Ivory Black | Titanium White |

Making a colour tower like this is a great way to practise mixing warm lights and cool shadows. It's rare that we achieve this lively effect by simply adding black and white to a colour. Each block is mixed separately and adjusted to keep the illusion of light and shade consistent from the top of the tower to the bottom.

This cityscape was painted on a sunny September morning in Manchester, England. It was completed in about two hours, by which time the 'golden hour' of light had faded and the shadows were in different positions.

The thing that grabs me and makes me paint is often not the subject itself, but an effect of light or simple blocks of colour. Here the exciting thing was the colour of the buildings against the dull blue sky. I wanted to include some of that fabulous orange on the right but realized that it could easily take all the attention if it was too large a chunk of colour. I decided to crop all but a small slice of it on the right-hand side.

For this project, you may copy my painting but if you prefer to work from your own photo, try to find an image that has clearly distinguished areas of light and shade.

WARM LIGHTS AND COOL SHADOWS

This 'colour tower' (right) is made from swatches of colour taken from the finished painting. On the right-hand side the blocks are bathed in warm morning sunlight, which has an orange tinge. On the left are colours from the shadow area of the painting. These are all darker and cooler, tending towards purple-blue.

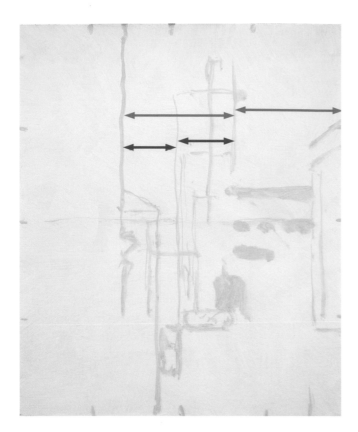

STAGE 1

This project is similar to the previous one in requiring a direct approach within a limited timescale. Do only as much drawing as is required to place the large colour shapes. Remember to look for matching measurements in the subject and make them match in your painting too.

By the time I had got even this much drawing done, the shadows had moved significantly. It is usually best to stick to the initial impression a scene makes upon you; a clear tonal plan (see page 51) at the outset can really help with this.

STAGE 2

This is go-for-the-jugular painting. Use your large brushes to pile on the thick paint right from the start. Too many times I have finished a painting only to wish I had used more paint.

In colour mixes, include your warmest colours (yellows and cadmium red) in the areas of warm sunlight and your coolest (blue and crimson) in the shadows. The glass building in the upper right is a mix of viridian and white with some yellow ochre to keep it warm. The sky colour, being a neutral (neither cool nor warm), is a mixture of a cool colour (blue) and a warm colour (cadmium red) plus white.

Hold a paintbrush up to your perspective lines (shown in white) to check that they all converge on the vanishing point (the red dot). The signs and ledge on the left-hand building did not line up, so in the next stage I will have to make those angles steeper.

Perspective also affects people. Of course, people further away appear smaller, but in general their heads are on a similar level – close to our own eye level. Their feet, however, will be at varying heights.

STAGE 3

At this stage you may begin to introduce lines and details using smaller brushes. As you do so, don't forget to keep the warm light areas distinct from the cool shadows. To simplify the effect, you can even paint details of the right-hand buildings lighter and warmer than they actually appear. Leave a gap of canvas to prevent the dull sky colour from muddying the delicate orange of the building. This will be filled in later with a small brush and orange paint.

Now is a good time to check your perspective. The essential effect of perspective is that things get smaller and closer together as they go into the distance. This includes the parallel lines of buildings, which all get closer together (converge) until they disappear at a vanishing point. This point always sits on our eye level (yellow line). Imagine standing in a flood up to your eyes. The level of the water would be your eye level. If you were to sit down, the flood would drain to give you a new eye level.

Tip
Don't be a slave to correctness. Nobody cares if you paint the correct number of windows in a building – except perhaps the owner.

STAGE 4

We are about three-quarters of the way through the painting and there are hardly any details. It's easy to panic and start adding things to make it look more finished. In my opinion, this is the time when a mirror is at its most useful. You may think that stopping to look in the mirror will slow you down. On the contrary, it will tell you what is essential and you can leave out the rest.

Any details we add at this stage will make the subject a bit clearer, but can also be used to balance the colours in the painting. This balancing of colours is not an exact science and you shouldn't worry about getting it right or wrong, but it is true that echoing colours throughout the painting helps to tie it all together.

The strongest colours in this painting are the orange building on the right and the yellow square in the centre. If these were the only notes of those colours, they would feel isolated from the rest of the picture. The lines on the road, painted in duller versions of those colours, help to connect them to the rest of the painting.

Use a lift-off highlight to create the glow of the street lamp.

STAGE 5

A city isn't a city without people, but you only need one or two to give a sense of life. I encourage you to suggest the overall shape of people with as few brushmarks as possible. If you are painting on the street, glance at a walking figure for less than a second to fix the shape in your mind. You can combine parts from different glimpsed figures into one person. Keep the legs soft and don't paint the feet distinctly or the person will look static.

Remember that you can omit people or move them around to improve your painting. You can see in stage 2 that I thought of having a large central figure. This person commanded too much attention, stopping us in the middle of the painting, so was made into a dustbin!

The shadow side of the distant building was too defined, so the handle of the brush was used to scratch a quick squiggle through it. With the edges broken, it is no longer coming forward in space and the scratches might even suggest windows.

The lit street lamp is painted using the halo effect (see page 53). Start with a large dash of orange, then mix a large pile of yellow and use the lift-off technique (see page 23) to get a nice blob of paint on your brush. This is laid in the middle of the orange dash for that glowing effect.

Secret garden

Painting this charming subject under more constant light gives us time
to concentrate on subtleties of composition and paint surface. Just beware
of the temptation to include every leaf and brick!

COLOURS NEEDED

Phthalo
Blue

Viridian
Hue

Cadmium
Yellow
Pale

Yellow
Ochre

Burnt
Sienna

Permanent
Alizarin
Crimson

Cadmium
Red

Ivory
Black

Titanium
White

Photo of the scene. In the finished painting the distant trees and grass area have been enlarged and the ivy has been moved.

The previous two paintings were made in quickly changing light conditions – setting sun and morning sunshine. Secret Garden was painted on an overcast day when the light remained constant for longer periods. Such grey days allow the artist to spend longer on the painting and include more detail. The challenge is to find enough contrast and colour to keep the painting lively. When we have more time, we also need to know when to stop.

The subject is close to my heart because it is where my wife Lindsey and I got married. It was painted as a wedding present for some dear friends who were getting married there too.

The view is framed so that the gate is off-centre to avoid boring symmetry. The focal point – the birch trees – are placed near the upper-left third of the canvas. I wanted a little bit of floor in front of the gate visible as an entrance into the painting – creating the feeling that you can walk through the gate into the bright courtyard.

The tonal plan (see page 51) was pretty simple: light courtyard, medium-tone walls and dark gateway. Try to stick to this arrangement even as you add more details.

This blurred photo represents the tonal plan I have in mind.

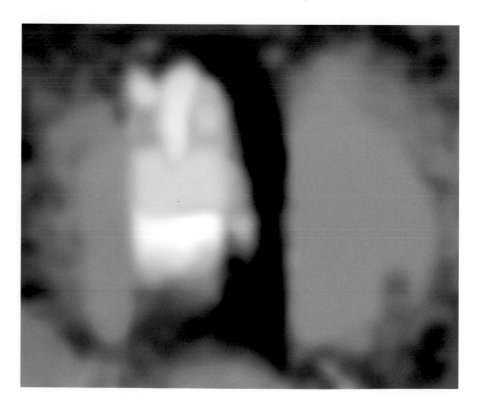

STAGE 1

The board is toned with a wash of burnt sienna, wiped gently with a rag. This warm ground looks great peeping through subjects containing lots of cool colours or greens.

A quick line drawing with diluted brown is followed by establishing our lightest light. Not pure white though. The left side of the birch has a touch of pinky purple (crimson and blue) while the shadow side has a hint of orange.

Very quickly, we want to darken the colour of the wall, without obliterating the ground colour. Dilute the paint a lot and use a No. 6 brush to make loose strokes in all directions, holding the brush underhand. Add more crimson and a touch of blue for the areas under the ivy.

STAGE 2

The birch trees are a lovely symbol for the bride and groom, but they felt crushed at the top of the painting. So I moved the trees down, along with the section of grass, to give them more space.

The bright grass (yellow, viridian and white) is scumbled (see page 25) across the surface, leaving a few specks of orange ground showing through. Like pure white, pure black must be used sparingly or it has a deadening effect. Here it is used for the gateway, but is varied by the addition of other colours in the other dark areas.

STAGE 3

Unlike the warm light of the previous paintings, today's overcast sky gives a cooler light falling on the whole scene. To convey this, the light area of the path has a hint of purple in it. It is put on thickly with the palette knife.

The ivy and bricks are created with short commas of thick paint. It's great if the colours are not fully mixed before applying them, as in the ivy leaves to the right of the door.

Individual strokes of unmixed paint for the ivy and bricks.

More varied spacing improves the composition of the painting.

STAGE 4

In a longer painting session such as this, taking a break can help you see your composition with fresh eyes. Clean off your palette and refresh your paint blobs, resisting the urge to glance at your painting. Turn your painting upside down, stand back as far as you can and look at it in a mirror.

This process helped me decide to remove the hanging ivy on the right of the gateway. I later realized that this improves the spacing of the vertical lines. It's good to trust the mirror, even if you don't understand what it's telling you at the time.

Don't be afraid to remove paint as well as put it on. At this stage a large amount of textured paint is removed with the side of the palette knife. The resulting surface is perfectly evocative of the old brick wall in a way that would have been impossible through simply adding more paint. Use the tip of the knife to scratch some tendrils in the lower right.

Dashes of paint used to suggest the bars of the gate.

STAGE 5

So far, we have been making strong and decisive changes to the painting. Now that we have settled on a final composition, it's tempting to go to town with the details. Be careful. Fiddling is a surefire way to lose the lively bits of orange ground peeping through and the exciting textures we created through scraping back.

A good cheat if you do overwork things and lose the ground colour is to mix up something to imitate it (yellow, red and a touch of white) and dab it in here and there. I may just have done this in the painting, but I'm not going to tell you all my secrets.

The iron gate is a complicated bit of drawing you needn't lose sleep over. If you wear glasses, take them off and paint the bits of colour that you see. This sounds over-simplistic, but the requirement is really only that you trust your eyes. Neither the dark green lines for some of the bars, nor the blue-grey at the left edge of the gate make any sense logically. Yet this is what my shortsighted eyes saw and, actually, they do a perfect job of describing the gate without painting every bar.

The bricks too could have taken a week of diligent work. Instead, defining a few edges and varying the colour of the bricks gives a fairly decent impression of old brickwork, without losing all the texture underneath.

A few flicks of colour to indicate fallen leaves in the gateway enliven this dark passage of paint, but we are in danger of fiddling now, so let's scratch in a signature and call it a day.

Sky

In this project you will paint the sky in an indirect technique.
That is, you will prepare a white surface with textures, leave it to dry,
then use glazes and velaturas to create rich textural effects.

COLOURS NEEDED

Phthalo Blue	Viridian Hue	Yellow Ochre	Burnt Sienna	Permanent Alizarin Crimson	Titanium White

The sky is quite unlike any other subject we can paint. It is a constantly evolving abstract painting with new formations, colours and moods appearing every few minutes. Sit and look out of a window on a windy day and you will see exactly what I mean.

This painting features various kinds of clouds in different layers of the sky. Those closest to us, (the tiny blue-grey ones in the finished painting) move fastest, scuttling across the foreground. Spectacular cumulus clouds (those familiar cotton-wool balls) are lit by the noonday sun high above us. These goliaths move at a more lumbering pace – still too fast if you're trying to draw them – but are constantly turning, edges breaking off, and making new cloud formations.

High in the sky, where the atmosphere is coldest, the delicate textures of cirrus and cirrocumulus stay still for longer. At this height, the freezing exhausts of jet planes create cloud formations in a category all by themselves: vapour trails.

REFERENCE PHOTO

Photography is an excellent tool for freezing the motion of the sky, allowing us to study the exact shapes of clouds. Even so, you will notice many differences between my reference photo and the finished painting. Aware of the fact that photography cannot capture the subtle, airy colours of clouds, I based my colours on previous studies done directly from the sky.

A subject such as this gives us great flexibility in how we apply the paint. We can invent shapes to suit our composition because clouds can be almost any shape anyway. Rather than trying to copy the exact shapes and textures of my painting, allow the paint to have a life of its own, echoing the natural movement of clouds.

So long as you bear in mind the following general effects, you will get away with adventurous paintwork:

- The tops of the clouds are the most brightly lit.
- Shapes of clouds get flatter and thinner towards the horizon.
- Blue sky gets lighter and more turquoise towards the horizon.
- Cloud colours get warmer towards the horizon.

A sliver of landscape at the base of the painting gives scale to the clouds and by its relative darkness can make the sky look lighter. I prefer to keep the details vague, so that it does not depict a specific location, but you may add any landscape you wish.

Tip
You can paint great cloud shapes using photos, but when it comes to mixing accurate sky colours, nothing beats looking at the sky itself.

A summer sky over Lytham St Annes, England.

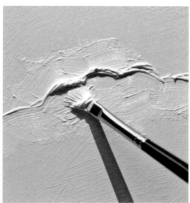

Painting up to a ridge of paint makes it more pronounced.

STAGE 1

Using only white paint, have some fun seeing what textures you can create as you build up the lightest areas of the clouds. You may use brushes, the palette knife, your fingers or any tool you like. In the upper clouds, try some scumbling (see page 25), dragging the paint lightly over the surface. I used the palette knife for the flat bottoms of the clouds closer to the horizon. You could use the lift-off technique (see page 23) to create the silver lining on the very tops of the clouds. These ridges of paint can be made even finer by painting up to them with a brush.

You can manipulate the paint for as long as you like, scraping off and reapplying until you have achieved a variety of textures. This stage must be left to dry before proceeding. About a week should be long enough in a warm environment.

STAGE 2

We will be using glazes to introduce colour over the white textured ground. Dip a large brush into your painting medium (solvent and linseed oil mixed) and make a pool of it on your clean palette. Mix in some burnt sienna, then add a touch of blue to dull the colour. If the glaze is too watery, add more paint.

Apply this glaze to all the cloud areas, going slightly over the edges into the blue sky region. The image shows a freshly applied glaze. Next, you will use a rag to gently wipe the glaze until it looks like the clouds in stage 3. Keep turning the rag to a clean side so that the raised surfaces of paint become clean, leaving paint in the crevices. If you are unhappy with your glaze, it can easily be completely removed using a rag dipped in solvent.

STAGE 3

Blue sky transitions from a dark purple-blue high up to a lighter, more turquoise blue at the horizon. To convey this, start by mixing a pure blue glaze. Apply this into the middle section of the blue sky, then add a little crimson into the mix for the higher areas. Clean off your paintbrush, then add a little viridian to the blue for the lower section. Keep turning the rag as you wipe the glaze and press more firmly on the lower area of the sky so that it becomes lighter than the upper regions.

STAGE 4

We can create variety in the cloud area by using milky glazes known as velaturas (see page 27). The starting point for all four velaturas is light grey (**1**), made by adding white, blue, crimson and burnt sienna to a pool of painting medium.

Apply your velaturas with a No. 4 brush, using the paintbrush in a messy fashion. Add more burnt sienna to your initial mix to create a warm velatura, suitable for closer to the horizon (**2**). Adding white gives a lighter mix for the higher clouds (**3**). A final, less diluted mix with more blue and crimson gives the darker colour of the foreground floaters (**4**).

For the delicate high clouds, return to undiluted paint. Use the knife to mix a blue slightly lighter and greyer than the sky. With some of this mix on the back of the knife, gently glide it over the upper sky area and see where the paint catches the raised surface. The effect is more varied and convincing than trying to paint each tiny cloud.

With this same mix, stamp the edge of the knife on the canvas to create the straight thin lines of vapour trails (upper left). Mine are a bit fuzzy at this stage but get sharpened up later. The final job for this stage is to refresh the sparkle in the highlights of the clouds using thick white paint and just a touch of yellow ochre.

Mixing four velaturas.

*Balancing the diagonals
(above left & right).*

STAGE 5

If you feel that your painting is too cluttered, use the sky colour to paint over some clouds. You will notice the textured surface at the top of my painting where I have removed a cloud. This remaining texture is known as 'pentimento', Italian for repentance or a change of mind.

Look for the main diagonals in your painting. If they are all tilting one way, you may need to introduce or strengthen some opposing diagonals to restore the sense of balance. At stage 4, my strongest diagonals are sloping upwards to the right (see the white lines). I begin to restore the balance by softening the edges of the upper left cloud. I then adjust the dark grey foreground clouds to slope down to the right (see the lower pink line). Finally, I strengthen the downward sloping vapour trail by stamping on more paint with the edge of the knife (see the upper pink line).

The landscape is painted with the No. 1 brush, combining touches of brown, green and ochre. Some bluer sections hint at water. Include a few verticals to break the horizon line. I placed my main vertical roughly two-thirds from the left. This lower section of the painting might be disturbed by a big signature, so consider one of the top corners. I opt for the top right and use a subtle colour very close to that of the sky.

FOCUS ON
Painting People

Painting another person is the ultimate challenge and also, in my opinion, the most exciting thing you can do with a paintbrush. Don't avoid it any longer or you won't know what you're missing!

I recommend two projects: a self-portrait painted looking in a mirror and a painting of another person from a photo. If, like me, you get hooked on painting people, you should eventually look for opportunities to draw and paint people 'from life', that is, from an actual person as opposed to from photos. This gives the strongest emotional connection to the sitter.

In the meantime, you can rapidly improve your drawing skills by buying a small sketchbook and filling it with scribbles of people on the bus, watching TV or waiting at the doctor's. Local life-drawing classes give you the chance to draw somebody keeping still for longer.

Techniques

The techniques we use for drawing people are exactly the same as those we use for drawing a still life or any other subject. Why then do we find painting people more difficult? The problems arise because our minds interfere with what we see.

In our artwork as children, and even as adults, we tend to exaggerate the most significant features while making less interesting body parts smaller. This is why the most common error in drawing the face is positioning the eyes too high. The eyes, nose and mouth are most interesting, so we enlarge them to fill the face.

We know that the face is symmetrical. When faced with a subject looking over to one side (known as a three-quarter view), we have a tendency to disbelieve our eyes. We instinctively 'correct' what we see, dragging the features back towards the middle of the face.

Knowing a few of these pitfalls can help you get your figure paintings right. The main thing, however, is learning to treat a person just like any other subject and tricking your mind into drawing shapes, not the subject.

The best technique for seeing a person as simply shapes is to turn them upside down. This is unpopular with real models but a photograph has no objections. With the photo and your painting upside down (or sideways; that works too) you can copy shapes with surprising accuracy. Don't forget, whichever way around it is, to compare your subject to the painting using the mirror (see page 15).

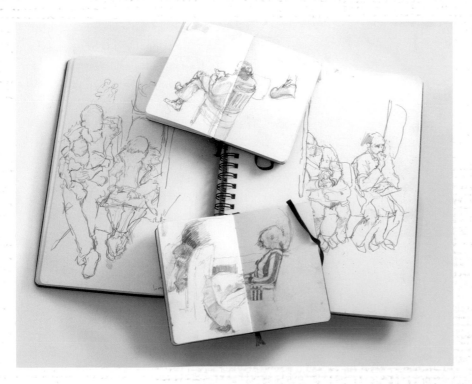

Improve your drawing skills by sketching whenever you can.

In my first painting of Zoe (**1A**), I made a few common mistakes. My second attempt (**1B**) came out much better. When painting the figure, we tend to start with the head and work down. In my first painting, I made the head too large, then squashed the legs to fit them onto the canvas. For my second attempt, I started by roughly placing the shape of the whole figure and chair comfortably within the rectangle.

Because the top half of a person is more interesting, we tend to paint it bigger than the lower half. In my second painting of Zoe, I overcame this problem by using the measuring technique (see page 14) to locate a halfway point on the figure (see the white arrows). Drawing two half-people is much easier than one whole one. The same measurement turned horizontally gave me the width of the model and chair.

In my first painting, Zoe appears too upright. To keep the correct alignment in my second attempt, I used a paintbrush to align the neck with the back of the foot (see the blue line). Positioning the feet of people and chairs can also be tricky. In my first painting, they landed level with the base of the painting. Holding a brush to match the angles (see the red line) helped me see their positions more clearly.

The setting is vital to the success of a figure painting. The cast shadows in the second painting create a much clearer sense of light and connect the figure to the space. The background in the first is painted almost up to the figure but does not go behind her in the way it does in the second. There is also more harmony of colour in the second painting, with a balance of intense and muted colours being used. Finally, my signature needed a little taming to stop it distracting from the subject.

Two paintings of the same model, one of which shows more careful observation.

1A

1B

Self-portrait

*For practising portraiture there is no better model than the one in the mirror.
Not only does he or she only take breaks when you do, they won't be offended if
you don't achieve a perfect likeness. In fact, you will be painting with a palette knife,
so the aim is a well-painted head as opposed to a detailed portrait.*

COLOURS NEEDED

| Phthalo Blue | Viridian Hue | Cadmium Yellow Pale | Yellow Ochre | Burnt Sienna | Permanent Alizarin Crimson | Cadmium Red | Ivory Black | Titanium White |

For this exercise, you will use a lot of paint. If you are concerned about cost, you may consider using student-grade paints even for the cadmium colours.

I'm sure you will find painting your own image in a mirror both more bearable and more useful than copying my self-portrait. Tell yourself before you start that this one is a learning experience for yourself, not to show to your friends. It's unlikely you will be maintaining an elegant smile for the hours it takes to complete the painting.

SETTING UP

Before you start, experiment with your position in relation to the mirror and the light source. As you do this, half close your eyes to see the changing pattern of light and shade on your face. I positioned myself to have the light of a window coming from one side. If possible, have your canvas angled to receive good light. Keep the background simple on a small painting such as this.

Position the mirror and the canvas (on the easel) next to each other, then look directly at the canvas. Keeping your head locked, just swivel your eyes to look in the mirror and then back towards your canvas. Maintaining your head in one position and just moving your eyes makes it much easier to compare your beautiful subject to your masterpiece in progress.

You will still need to move your head to look down at your palette. Returning to the correct position is easier if you take note of an aspect of your face such as how much of your far ear you can see. I used the little triangle of wall colour caught in my glasses as my anchor.

Measuring with the brush is a little confusing when looking in a mirror as you see two hands and two brushes – one real and one reflected. The trick is to decide which one you are going to measure with and ignore the other. We know that the eyes are generally positioned about halfway between the chin and the top of the head. If we can find two such matching measurements, we can avoid the most common error in portrait painting, placing the eyes too high in the head.

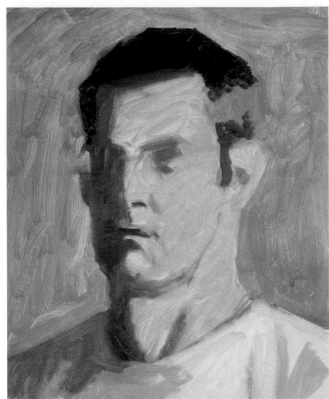

STAGE 1

Try to see your head as a series of flat shapes. Imagine your face, hair and neck as three adjoining countries, each with a distinctive outline. With a No. 2 round brush, begin drawing these three flat shapes, aiming to capture their relative sizes and the way they interlock. Use diluted paint and a delicate colour (I used yellow ochre with a touch of red and white) which will not muddy subsequent layers. Erase mistakes with a rag dipped in solvent and redraw as many times as you like.

Include the shapes of your shoulders, going right to the edges of the canvas. Hold your brush to match the angle of a shoulder, then transfer this angle to your painting.

With a slightly diluted mix of burnt sienna, black and yellow ochre, indicate the pattern of shadow shapes which appear on your face. Don't be alarmed by how dark this colour looks. You are seeing it in relation to the white canvas.

STAGE 2

Using diluted paint, wash in the colour for the light side of your face (for me it is yellow ochre, red and white). For the remaining areas of hair, clothing and background, aim for a similar tonal value to what you see, but take some liberties with the colour. Anything peeping through the thicker layers on top will look better than the glaring white canvas.

Tip

Mark the positions of your features, but don't get enticed into details. There is no point painting a perfect eye until you know that it's in the right place.

Mix generous quantities of flesh colours with the knife.

Tip

Apart from the obvious area of the lips, the parts of the face which appear redder are usually those which feel cold in winter – ears, nose and cheeks.

STAGE 3

Flesh colours vary drastically according to the complexion of the individual and the lighting conditions. Here I show you eight mixtures and where I use them on the face.

For basic Caucasian flesh colour, use white, yellow ochre and red (**1**). This is the starting point for lots of the other mixtures. Add more red and orange for warmer areas of flesh such as the nose and cheek (**2**). The reddest flesh colour, found in the ear, is the previous mix with crimson and blue added (**3**).

Duller colours (known as neutrals) occur in the beard area. My dark neutral is made of the basic flesh colour plus viridian and orange (**4**). The light neutral (**5**) is mixed to the same tonal value as the basic flesh colour but has some of the dark neutral, plus burnt sienna and white added.

The flesh colours are mixed thoroughly to a unified colour. When it comes to the background mixtures, feel free to dip the tip of the palette knife into lots of different colours and not mix them fully. As you apply this unmixed colour to the painting, it creates exciting 'broken colour' effects.

A warm shadow colour is made of burnt sienna with yellow ochre and white (**6**). Adding crimson and more burnt sienna gives the darkest shadow (**7**).

STAGE 4

Painting with the palette knife can feel awkward at first, but keep using it for as long as you can. It forces you to simplify and leads to freshness of marks. If you do need to measure and make a few correcting marks for the position of things, use a No. 2 round brush.

Here I measured the position of my eye using the paintbrush and found that I had it way too far to the left. I marked the new position using the brush and am in the process of moving the nose and mouth to the right to fit in with the new eye position. It's never too late for major corrections.

If the edge between the head and the background is kept too rigid, it can look like a cutout. To overcome this, colours from the background are dragged into the hair and some colour from the cheek is lightly dragged into the background.

Tip
Rather than black, use dark red for the nostrils and ear cavities to keep the feeling of life in the portrait.

STAGE 5

Beware of using too much white in the flesh colours as you make your final corrections. Keep the colours rich and reserve your white for the highlights at the end. Even here, my highlights have a little purple mixed into them.

In painting the eyes, the key is to paint only what you see. Particularly avoid details and highlights in a shaded eye. Look how little information I have given about mine. To avoid a staring look, make sure the top section of the iris is covered by the eyelid. The 'whites' of the eyes are rarely white. In most circumstances, a greyish colour to the same tonal value as the flesh looks much better.

Oil paint dries on the surface first, forming a skin. Thickly applied paint such as this may be touch dry within a week, but will remain wet under the surface. Be careful not to squash the impasto by putting anything against the face of the painting for a month or so. You can test if the paint has dried solid by gently pushing it with your finger. If it moves, it is still wet underneath.

Seated Figure

This project introduces you to a range of techniques that make figure painting from photos far less daunting. You will be using a limited palette to maintain harmony. This is particularly useful in reducing the number of colour choices you have, leaving you free to concentrate on the essential qualities of drawing and tonality.

COLOURS NEEDED

Yellow Ochre	Burnt Sienna	Permanent Alizarin Crimson	Ivory Black	Titanium White

LIMITED PALETTE

Swedish artist Anders Zorn did most of his paintings using only black, white, yellow ochre and red. I am being generous in adding a fifth colour, burnt sienna.

Place your colours around the edge of your palette in the order shown. Just as with the full palette, it's a good idea to pre-mix the secondary colours (green and purple) before you start so that you have clean versions of these. You could also make a dull brown from burnt sienna, yellow ochre and black.

PAINTING FROM
BLURRED TO CLEAR

When painting the figure from life, I invariably wear an old pair of glasses, which only partially correct my vision. The lack of detail is useful in allowing me to see the subject as simple blocks of colour. Only at the end do I trust myself to see the details, at which point I realize how few are actually needed to finish the painting.

In this project we are painting Alice from photos that mimic that exact process. The initial blurred image encourages us to work with large general shapes of colour, gradually building towards smaller shapes and clearer focus. If you are lucky enough to have poor eyesight, you can remove your glasses for the same effect. To blur your photos in Photoshop, use filters such as Palette Knife, Paint Daubs and Blur.

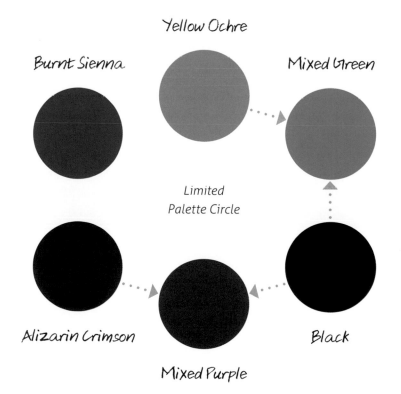

Yellow Ochre

Burnt Sienna

Mixed Green

Limited
Palette Circle

Alizarin Crimson

Black

Mixed Purple

Upside-down, blurred image with grid lines.

STAGE 1

Use a large brush to cover the surface of the canvas with a dull brown mix. Gently wipe this with a rag, then either leave it to dry overnight or paint on it immediately. Grid your canvas with half and quarter lines using pencil. We are working from an upside-down image to help us concentrate on the things which matter at this stage – the large shapes and colours. If we can forget that it's a person altogether, that's ideal. Try to give equal attention to all areas of the painting. Beginners have a tendency to worry the figure to death while neglecting the space they are sat in. Painting the negative shapes and colours can really help your figure – and it's much easier!

Using the grid lines to guide you, block in your lightest lights and darkest darks. Add some crimson to your blacks to keep them rich. Sometimes when working with a limited palette, it's possible that you may not be able to mix the exact colours of your subject. This does not matter. What matters is that the strongest versions of your colours are used in the right place. In this instance, Alice's blouse and the flower are the strongest orange notes in the subject, so for these we use pure yellow ochre with burnt sienna. Nothing else in the painting is allowed to be as purely orange as these. The wall and her hair colour are similar but duller.

Tip
When painting things with feet, like people or chairs, it's tempting to make them parallel with the bottom of the canvas. Hold your paintbrush horizontally to see which one is actually lowest and by how much.

STAGE 2

We now introduce the strongest notes of purple and green. In the process of painting, it's easy to lose your positioning grid lines. You can restate them by scratching through the paint with the wrong end of your brush.

The subject is lit by overhead fluorescent lights, meaning that all the upward-facing planes are light, while the vertical planes are darker. Alice's forearm and shoulder are facing upwards, while her bicep is vertical, so is slightly darker. Compare the top plane of the suitcase and bed (on the right) to their side planes to see how light affects everything in the same way.

The head and torso area, subdivided to help with proportions.

STAGE 3

Soft edges allow the eye to keep moving through the painting while hard edges stop the eye. In painting a person, we need to pay careful attention to the rendering of the head, but many other areas can be more loosely defined, with soft edges.

To achieve this balance of focus, firstly use torn kitchen towel, dragged through the paint, to soften the whole image. It may take a little courage to soften your entire figure painting, especially if it looks OK, but it usually pays off with a more atmospheric image.

Another fun way to soften the image is to stamp your fingers in the paint in one part of the painting, then place them in another area. This helps to echo colours throughout the painting and can be seen in the lower left corner, where fingerprints break up the boring colour of the floor.

Having softened the painting, use pencil to restate some of the grid lines. In the area of the face, divide the grid into smaller rectangles to help with the proportions.

A clearer image, divided into smaller rectangles in the head area.

Developing the planes of the face.

STAGE 4

At this stage we can work from a clearer photo to create more structure, especially in the upper body. Every now and then, work with the photo and painting upside down, especially when painting the head, and don't forget to compare them in the mirror. Keep moving around the whole painting and leave some soft edges.

Working from photos, it's hard to know when to stop. Just because you can keep adding details doesn't mean you should. If you have captured an aspect of the subject, that is plenty for one painting.

Shoppers in the Rain

This final project combines many of the techniques you have already learned in order to create the impression of moving figures at twilight. You may prefer to copy my finished painting directly but there are lessons to be learned in following the changes that occur along the way. We will be delving into warm and cool light, adventurous paint techniques and the balancing of colours in your composition.

COLOURS NEEDED

| Phthalo Blue | Viridian Hue | Cadmium Yellow Pale | Yellow Ochre | Burnt Sienna | Permanent Alizarin Crimson | Cadmium Red | Ivory Black | Titanium White |

MAKING CHANGES

The changes an artist makes to their subject reveals their personal viewpoint. Over time you will gain confidence in making such adjustments. For me, the two friends out shopping are the main subject, so they are given more space by moving the figures on their left. The colours of the background are changed to an overall cool light I remember from walking around town at this time of day. To make this possible, the perspective of the buildings is adjusted to reveal an area of blue sky.

From the complex lighting of the photo I have emphasized two main areas of warm light to contrast the blue atmosphere: the brightly lit shop window and the pinkish light (probably a streetlight) falling on the lady with the pink umbrella.

BALANCING YOUR COMPOSITION

You will know by now that creating a painting is not just about copying the subject that you see before you. Creating a balanced composition requires that you trust your natural sense of what looks right and be willing to make the changes that occur to you. Here are some more handy techniques for seeing your work with fresh eyes:

- Hide the reference photo and just work on the painting for a while.
- Take a photo of the painting on your phone and look at the photo.
- Prop the painting in progress in a prominent place, then look at it in a casual way.
- Ask a friend. You don't have to take their suggestions, but it certainly gives you another viewpoint.

- Do a small drawing of your painting as it is, then practise changes on your drawing rather than on the painting itself.
- To test if an area of the painting is helping or hindering, close one eye and cover up the area with your thumb.
- If you find yourself making endless changes, start another painting exactly the same as the first, then work on them in tandem. Allow them to go in different directions. You may end up with two for the price of one!

Tip
No matter how nicely painted, one little part of the painting can never be as important as the whole.

Compare the photo to the finished painting to see which elements have been changed.

STAGE 1

Tone the canvas using a dull red made from crimson mixed with touches of black, white, blue and yellow ochre. Dilute the paint and use a large brush to apply the paint in a messy fashion. If you are using a grid, scratch the lines into the wet paint using the wrong end of the brush. Some of this warm ground may remain in the final painting as a contrast to the predominantly cool subject.

The subject is liable to undergo many changes, so don't invest lots of time in a detailed drawing. Use a No. 4 brush and reddish-brown paint to indicate where the darks may be. In the painting of Alice (the previous project), we were quite sure of where the darks would be, so we painted them full strength right from the start. Here we are feeling our way, so we use a gentler dark, which is easier to erase or paint over if need be.

Simplify the spotty umbrella to a single colour, unless you like spots. Each plane is distinguished from the next by being a slightly different colour. The sky is applied thickly with the palette knife, allowing specks of the ground to show through.

The bright red dot is a vanishing point. It is at my eye level and around the same height as the other people's eyes. It allows us to invent buildings and keep them in the correct perspective. All the diagonal lines in the buildings and pavement will point to this spot.

Thick paint and a halo of warm colour are used to convey glowing light.

STAGE 2

Having established some lights and darks, you can now move on to the areas of strongest colour. Use big brushes and thick paint for the brightly lit shop window. Squint your eyes to see how everything in the window is lighter than everything outside (with the exception of the girl's coat). Use red and pink to create a colour halo around the edges of the window, creating the effect of glowing light.

The pavement on the right, which reflects the sky colour, is made from two large piles of blue (one darker, one lighter). They are applied unmixed with the palette knife to suggest patchy puddles. Overall, the colour reflected in the pavement should be darker and duller than the sky itself. The same principle is followed for the reflection of the shop window.

The distant buildings are painted with decisive strokes directly into the wet paint of the sky. The closeness of the colours creates a sense of space.

STAGE 3

There are lots of changes at this stage. The umbrella was too similar to the colour of the coat, so was changed to pink. This change in turn made the coat too obviously the focal point, so the light-pink shop sign was introduced above the figures to draw the eye away from this central focal point.

The dark-haired lady's head was coinciding with the vertical of the shop window behind her. The area of the window was extended to prevent this.

The sky was simplified with the palette knife and thicker pinks applied in the shop window. Now that we have settled where the dark areas will be (generally across the middle band of the painting), they are made darker. Solid black areas can look like holes in a painting, so a palette knife is scraped across the surface to 'open them up', revealing some of the texture of the board.

The huge amount of paint in the right foreground was distracting from more important areas, so was scraped off. Don't be afraid to improvise. Any tool or technique is fair game. I found a piece of wood lying around and used the end of it stamped in paint to create the textured pink area in the floor. See if you can invent some of your own techniques.

The effect achieved by scraping a piece of wood across the surface.

Tip
Removing paint can
be just as creative as
putting it on.

STAGE 4

Take a deep breath. The piece of wood I found is placed vertically and scraped
across the whole painting except the top-right quarter. Suddenly, it's much better!
The textures are more subtle, the colours have settled into a happy arrangement
and there is an exciting impression of movement.

Now all the painting needs is a little definition in the figures and the restraint to
not over-correct or we will lose the freshness of the impression. The legs are kept
soft-edged in places to maintain a sense of movement.

Don't be afraid to take such risks with your paintings and always take credit for
happy accidents. The little blob of yellow on the right was a fluke, but it perfectly
balances the larger shape of yellow on the left, so I'll take it.

Having followed some of the changes my painting went through, I hope you will
feel confident to interpret your own future subjects in a personal way.

Glossary

AERIAL PERSPECTIVE The effect in a landscape of distant things appearing lighter and bluer than close things.

ALLA PRIMA Technique of completing a painting in one go, before the paint dries.

COMPLEMENTARY COLOURS A pair of colours from opposite sides of the colour wheel. They enhance each other when placed side by side and kill each other when mixed.

COMPOSITION The arrangement of shapes, lines, colours and textures within a painting.

EARTH COLOURS Browns and muted colours.

FAT OVER LEAN The rule of using fatty paint (containing more linseed oil) over lean paint (containing less oil) in order to prevent cracking.

FIDDLING Adding unnecessary detail to a painting.

FOCAL POINT Area in the painting that first draws the viewer's eye through detail or contrast.

FROM LIFE Painting directly from a person, object or scene, as opposed to from photographs or drawings.

GLAZE Thin transparent layer of paint used to modify an underlying colour.

GROUND A layer of primer applied to the support to stop the oil from sinking in. Can be white (acrylic gesso) but can also be coloured and textured using oil paint.

IMPASTO Thick paint.

LIMITED PALETTE Deliberately reducing the number of colours used to maintain harmony in the painting.

LOCAL COLOUR The colour of an object itself, regardless of light or shade.

MATCHING MEASUREMENTS Technique of finding two identical distances in the subject which can be replicated in the painting.

MEDIUM A mixture of solvent and linseed oil.

NEGATIVE SHAPES Shapes around or between objects.

PLEIN-AIR PAINTING French term for outdoor painting.

REFLECTED LIGHT Light bouncing off a surface into the shadow side of an object.

RULE OF THIRDS Compositional concept of dividing the rectangle into thirds and placing major lines or subjects on these lines or junctions.

SGRAFFITO Scratching back through wet paint to reveal underlying colours.

SOLVENT Clear liquid used to dilute and clean oil paints.

TONAL PLAN A mental image of where the main light and dark areas of a painting will be.

TONAL VALUE (ALSO KNOWN AS TONE OR VALUE) Relative lightness or darkness of a colour.

TONKING Applying paper to the surface of a wet painting to remove paint.

TRANSPARENT PAINT Paints which allow light to travel through them and reflect back from the surface underneath. Suitable for glazing.

UNDERPAINTING First layers of paint, applied with the intention of being partially or completely covered.

VANISHING POINT All parallel lines converge on this point, which sits on your horizon line.

VELATURA A glaze that contains an opaque paint such as white.

VIEWFINDER Device with a rectangular hole for viewing the subject.

WET-IN-WET Technique of applying wet paint on top of or into wet paint.

About the Author

Norman Long BA MAFA studied at Blackpool and Fylde College, Newcastle University and the Pennsylvania Academy of Fine Arts. In addition to 13 solo shows, his work has featured in distinguished group exhibitions in the USA and throughout the UK, including the BP Portrait Award. He is a winner of the Royal Society of Portrait Painters' de Laszlo Award and Artist and Illustrator's Artist of the Year 2013.

A full-time artist and teacher since 1999, Norman says, "I love that I can spend time alone in the studio, making discoveries, and then share them with enthusiastic students." The independent Norman Long Studio School, based in Preston, was founded in 2012.

Norman lives in Lytham St Annes, England, with his American artist wife Lindsey and three budding artists: Boston, Jasper and Lennox Long.

Acknowledgements

A thousand thanks to… fantastic students and collectors who have kept me alive and sane since 1999; painting buddies, including the inimitable Northern Boys; generous and inspirational teachers, especially Norman Travis, Scott Noel and George Nick; the ever-patient staff of GMC Publications. Most of all, thanks go to my family for indulging my creative dream.

See more of Norman's work at www.normanlongartist.com

Index

To order a book, or to request a catalogue, contact:

GMC Publications Ltd

Castle Place, 166 High Street, Lewes, East Sussex

BN7 1XU, United Kingdom

Tel: +44 (0)1273 488005

www.gmcbooks.com